How to Spot Fake News and Verify Information Online

Essential Skills for Evaluating Sources and Detecting Lies in the Era of Misinformation

The Fix-It Guy

Copyright © The Fix-It Guy

Table of Contents

Introduction

Welcome, savvy truth-seekers, to a journey that will transform the way you navigate the vast sea of information swirling around us in the digital age! In a world where facts and fictions engage in an epic battle for our attention, I invite you to embark on a quest with me, through the pages of "How to Spot Fake News and Verify Information Online: Essential Skills for Evaluating Sources and Detecting Lies in the Era of Misinformation."

Imagine having a superpower that shields you from the relentless onslaught of fake news and deceitful information. Picture yourself confidently deciphering truth from fiction, effortlessly dismantling misleading headlines, and navigating the murky waters of social media with the precision of a seasoned detective. Intrigued? You should be!

In this book, we'll be your trusty sidekick, guiding you through the intricacies of information literacy in a way that's both enlightening and downright entertaining. We'll unveil the secrets of identifying red flags, mastering fact-checking techniques, and developing the kind of critical thinking skills that make misinformation quiver in fear.

Buckle up as we explore the wild terrain of social media, equipping you with the tools to sift through the noise and emerge unscathed. Whether you're a social media maven or just getting the hang of hashtags, we promise to make your online journey a breeze.

But hey, it's not just about debunking myths and separating fact from fiction, it's about empowering you. Together, we'll forge a shield of knowledge that renders misinformation powerless in your presence. And let's be honest, who wouldn't want to be the superhero of truth in this information-packed world?

So, grab your capes (or bookmarks), and let's embark on this adventure. "How to Spot Fake News and Verify Information Online" is not just a book; it's your ticket to becoming the Sherlock Holmes of the digital era, the Gandalf of information integrity. Are you ready to unravel the mysteries of the online realm? Your journey awaits!

Chapter 1

The Basics of Information Evaluation

Defining Credible Sources

Alright, my truth-seekers, let's kick things off by diving into the very foundation of our quest for truth, navigating the vast sea of information. Today, we're getting cozy with Chapter 1: The Basics of Information Evaluation. So grab your detective hat and let's roll!

You know what they say, "Trust but verify." And in this digital jungle, knowing how to identify credible sources is your trusty machete. No worries, we've got your back. Let's break this down into bite-sized, foolproof steps:

Step 1: The Who's Who

Start by choosing your battles wisely. Investigate the author or organization behind the information. Ask yourself, "Who are these folks, and what makes them the gurus of this topic?" If the author is a mystery, it might be time to put on your Sherlock cap.

Troubleshooting Tip: Mysterious author? Google them! Check out their credentials and see if they have a digital footprint. If not, proceed with caution.

Step 2: The Date Dance

Next, you'll want to check the publication date. Information, like fine wine, can get stale. Make sure you're sipping on the latest and greatest. Nobody wants to be caught spreading last season's news.

Troubleshooting Tip: No publication date in sight? Check for updates on the website or look for a more recent source. Stay current, my friends.

Step 3: The Who's Paying the Bill?

Now, let's talk biases. Every source has them, like your favorite aunt's secret lasagna recipe. Identify any potential biases and question why they might be serving up information with a side of perspective. It's all about balance, like doing a tightrope walk over a pit of misinformation.

Troubleshooting Tip: Feeling the bias but can't quite put your finger on it? Ask yourself, "Who benefits from this information?" It's like playing detective in your own mind.

Step 4: The Cross-Check Tango

We're not done yet! Cross-reference like it's a dance move. Compare information from multiple sources. It's like assembling a puzzle; the more pieces, the clearer the picture. If your sources are singing in harmony, you're on the right track.

Troubleshooting Tip: Conflicting info making your head spin? Dig deeper. Look for consensus among reliable sources and piece the puzzle together.

Step 5: The Reliability Rodeo

Lastly, evaluate the reliability of the platform. Is it a reputable source, or are they handing out information like flyers on a street corner? Trustworthy outlets have a track record; they're not one-hit wonders.

Troubleshooting Tip: Doubting the source's reliability? Check if they cite their own sources. It's like a credibility domino effect.

And there you have it! Defining credible sources is your first step in this epic journey. So go ahead, wield your machete, dance the tango, and ride that rodeo. Remember, the truth is out there, and you're well on your way to uncovering it!

Key Takeaways:
1. Investigate the author and their credentials.
2. Check the publication date to stay fresh.
3. Uncover biases like a detective on a mission.
4. Cross-reference information for a clearer picture.
5. Evaluate the reliability of the platform.

Next Steps:
Start practicing on a few articles or websites. Apply these steps like a pro detective, and soon, you'll be the master of source credibility!

Assessing Authorship and Expertise

Now that you've mastered the art of defining credible sources, let's dive deeper into the personas behind the words, assessing authorship and expertise. It's like choosing your team for a trivia night; you want the brainiacs, not the clueless wanderers. So, grab your detective magnifying glass, and let's get sleuthing!

Step 1: The Author's Credentials

Start by stalking, I mean, researching the author. Who are they, and what makes them the go-to guru on the topic? Look for those fancy academic degrees, years of experience, or any badges of honor they might have. It's not about being nosy; it's about ensuring you're getting advice from the seasoned pros.

Troubleshooting Tip: Author info feels elusive? Check the article's end for a bio or do a quick online search. Google is your friend, my dear detective.

Step 2: The Playground of Expertise

Now, let's assess the author's playground of expertise. Does their expertise match the topic at hand? You wouldn't trust a dentist to fix your car (unless they're a secret car genius, but that's another story). If they're claiming to be an expert, make sure they're not just swinging on the monkey bars of misinformation.

Troubleshooting Tip: Expertise not adding up? Verify their credentials on professional platforms or check if they've authored relevant publications.*1

Step 3: The Google Trail

Follow the author's Google trail like a digital bloodhound. Are they recognized by their peers or are they the lone wolf in the information wilderness? A reputable author leaves breadcrumbs, awards, recognitions, or at least a trail of articles. If they're a ghost in the digital realm, proceed with caution.

Troubleshooting Tip: Google not yielding results? Could be a red flag. Trustworthy authors usually leave a trace in the vast online wilderness.

Examining Publication Bias

Now, let's tackle another beast, publication bias. It's like that friend who only shares the good stuff on social media. We need to see the whole picture, not just the highlight reel.

Step 1: The Full Monty

Start by checking if the publication is showing the full Monty. Are they presenting a balanced view, or is it all sunshine and rainbows? Real information isn't afraid of a little rain; it stands strong in the storm of diverse perspectives.

Troubleshooting Tip: Too much sunshine? Look for alternative sources that provide a more well-rounded view of the topic.

Step 2: The Sneaky Omission

Watch out for the sneaky omission, a favorite move of biased publications. Are they conveniently leaving out crucial details that might alter your perspective? It's like trying to solve a mystery with half the clues.

Troubleshooting Tip: Missing pieces of the puzzle? Seek out other sources to fill in the blanks and complete the picture.

Step 3: The Diverse Cast

A reliable publication plays host to a diverse cast of voices. If it feels like a one-man show or a choir singing in unison, you might want to double-check. A symphony of perspectives is what we're after, not a monotone melody.

Troubleshooting Tip: Hearing a solo act? Explore other outlets to hear the harmonious blend of diverse opinions.

And there you have it, intrepid truth-seekers! Assessing authorship and sniffing out publication bias is your next challenge. So go ahead, put on your detective hat, scrutinize those authors, and unravel the hidden biases. The truth is counting on you!

Key Takeaways:
1. Investigate the author's credentials and expertise.
2. Verify the author's expertise in the specific topic.
3. Follow the Google trail for additional validation.
4. Check for publication bias by seeking a balanced view.
5. Watch out for sneaky omissions and ensure a diverse range of perspectives.

Chapter 2

Recognizing Red Flags

Identifying Sensationalism and Clickbait

Congratulations, truth-seekers! You've mastered the art of evaluating sources, and now, we're diving into the thrilling world of red flags. Buckle up; it's about to get wild. In Chapter 2, we're tackling the first set of red flag, Recognizing Red Flags: Identifying Sensationalism and Clickbait. Get ready for a rollercoaster ride through the realm of exaggerated headlines and flashy tactics!

Ever clicked on an article expecting groundbreaking news only to find yourself trapped in an endless slideshow of cat memes? Welcome to the dark side of the internet, sensationalism and clickbait. But fear not, my savvy friends; we're about to arm you with the skills to spot these red flags from a mile away.

Step 1: The Headline Hijinks
Start by giving the headline a side-eye. Is it screaming for attention, promising you the moon and stars? Sensational headlines are like carnival barkers trying to

lure you into the tent. Don't fall for the hype; real news doesn't need a circus.

Troubleshooting Tip: Feeling the hype? Strip away the sensationalism and focus on the core message. If it still sounds fishy, move on.

Step 2: The Emotional Rollercoaster

Sensational articles love playing with your emotions, anger, fear, joy, you name it. If you find yourself riding an emotional rollercoaster within the first few sentences, it's time to hit the emergency exit. Emotional manipulation is a telltale sign of a sensationalist piece.

Troubleshooting Tip: Emotions running high? Take a step back. Fact-check the emotional claims and see if they hold water.

Step 3: The Miracle Cure

Beware of articles promising miracle cures or groundbreaking solutions. Whether it's a magic weight-loss pill or the secret to eternal youth, sensationalism often disguises itself as the bearer of life-altering revelations. Spoiler alert: It's usually too good to be true.

Troubleshooting Tip: Smells like snake oil? Consult trusted sources or experts to validate any extraordinary claims.

Step 4: The Clickbait Dance

Now, let's talk about clickbait, the ninja of online deception. If the headline leaves you hanging like a cliffhanger from your favorite TV show, it's clickbait at work. They want you to take the bait, but you're too clever for that.

Troubleshooting Tip: Tempted to click? Pause and think. Is the information likely to be as exciting as the headline suggests? Spoiler: It rarely is.

Step 5: The Infamous Listicle Trap

Ah, the listicle, the slyest form of clickbait. "10 Shocking Facts You Won't Believe!" Brace yourself; it's probably a collection of trivial tidbits. They want you to keep clicking through the list, but you've got better things to do.

Troubleshooting Tip: Falling for the listicle trap? Skim through the entire list first. If it feels like a time-wasting expedition, save yourself and move on.

There you have it, champions of truth! Identifying sensationalism and clickbait is your mission should you choose to accept it. So, put on your red-flag goggles, dodge those clickbait bullets, and let the truth prevail!

Key Takeaways:
1. Beware of sensational headlines promising the moon.
2. Stay vigilant against emotional manipulation.
3. Question articles making miraculous claims.
4. Spot the clickbait dance and resist the temptation.
5. Avoid falling into the listicle trap.

Next Steps:
Practice these skills on your next scroll through social media or news websites. Soon, you'll be a red flag ninja, dodging sensationalism and clickbait like a pro!

Unmasking Biased Reporting

Welcome back, truth warriors! Now that you've conquered sensationalism and clickbait, it's time to unveil another layer of deception. In this chapter, we're diving into the intriguing world of biased reporting. Get ready to be the Sherlock Holmes of news, spotting bias with a magnifying glass and a smirk.

Biased reporting is like a chameleon, it blends in, waiting to pounce on your unsuspecting judgment. But fear not, dear readers; we're here to teach you the secrets of unmasking biased reporting.

Step 1: The Language Labyrinth

Start by dissecting the language used in the article. Is it neutral, or does it lean towards one side like a tower about to topple? Biased reporting often reveals itself through loaded words, framing issues in a way that nudges your opinion.

Troubleshooting Tip: Feeling the nudge? Swap out biased terms with neutral ones and see if the tone changes.

Step 2: The Source Shuffle

Investigate the source's reputation. Does it have a history of playing favorites or riding the bias train? Knowing the track record of your news source is like having a secret weapon against biased reporting.

Troubleshooting Tip: Suspecting bias? Explore alternative sources to get a more balanced perspective.

Step 3: The Selective Storytelling
Biased reporting loves a good game of hide and seek with facts. If an article conveniently omits crucial information or selectively tells the story, it's time to put on your investigative hat. Truth doesn't hide; it stands front and center.

Troubleshooting Tip: Missing puzzle pieces? Seek out additional sources to fill in the gaps.

Step 4: The Diverse Voices Check
Check for the diversity of voices in the reporting. Does it showcase a range of opinions, or is it a one-sided choir? A well-rounded piece welcomes diverse perspectives, while biased reporting prefers to echo a singular tune.

Troubleshooting Tip: Hearing a solo act? Explore other outlets for a harmonious blend of opinions.

And there you have it, my truth companions! Unmasking biased reporting is your next mission. So, grab your metaphorical magnifying glass, unravel the language labyrinth, and let the truth shine through!

Key Takeaways:
1. Analyze the language used in the article for neutrality.
2. Investigate the reputation of the news source.
3. Watch out for selective storytelling and missing information.
4. Check for a diverse range of voices in the reporting.

Next Steps:
Apply these steps to a few news articles. Soon, you'll be the expert at unmasking biased reporting, unveiling the truth one article at a time!

Spotting Manipulated Visuals and Media

Welcome back, digital detectives! In this chapter, we're donning our virtual spy glasses to uncover the secrets of manipulated visuals and media. It's time to separate the authentic from the altered, the real from the CGI. Ready to become a visual truth-seeker? Let's dive in!

In a world where seeing isn't always believing, it's crucial to develop a keen eye for manipulated visuals and media. Don't worry; we've got your back. Let's unveil the mysteries together.

Step 1: The Photoshop Detectives
Become a Photoshop detective by examining images closely. Look for inconsistencies, unusual shadows, or telltale signs of cloning. Photoshop can be a magician's wand, but we're here to reveal the sleight of hand.

Troubleshooting Tip: Suspicious of a perfect scene? Zoom in and scrutinize details. If it feels too flawless, it might be a Photoshop illusion.

Step 2: The Timeline Tango
Understand the timeline of visuals. Is that jaw-dropping image current or a blast from the past? Manipulators often recycle visuals to fit their narrative. A photo may be worth a thousand words, but context is priceless.

Troubleshooting Tip: Feeling a time warp? Search for the original source or check for related timestamps to unveil the truth.

Step 3: The Deepfake Dilemma

Watch out for deepfakes, digital masterpieces that blur the line between reality and fiction. If something looks too good (or bad) to be true, it might be an orchestrated performance. Deepfakes are the Hollywood actors of the digital realm.

Troubleshooting Tip: Suspicious of an uncanny resemblance? Use deepfake detection tools or consult experts for verification.

Step 4: The Video Verdict

Evaluate videos critically. Are they edited to tell a different story? Manipulators love to cut, paste, and rearrange scenes. Look for abrupt transitions, inconsistent lighting, or unusual jumps in the narrative.

Troubleshooting Tip: Smells like video manipulation? Compare multiple sources or analyze the metadata to get to the truth.

There you have it, vigilant observers! Spotting manipulated visuals and media is your latest superpower.

So, grab your digital magnifying glass, dissect those images, and let's embark on this visual journey together!

Key Takeaways:
1. Scrutinize images for inconsistencies and signs of Photoshop.
2. Investigate the timeline of visuals to ensure relevance.
3. Be wary of deepfakes and their digital disguises.
4. Critically evaluate edited videos for inconsistencies.

Next Steps:
Practice your newfound skills on a variety of images and videos. Soon, you'll be a visual detective, exposing manipulated media like a pro!

Chapter 3

Fact-Checking Techniques

Introduction to Fact-Checking

Greetings, truth-seekers! We've reached the heart of our journey, Chapter 3, where we unlock the secrets of Fact-Checking Techniques. In a world flooded with information, knowing how to separate fact from fiction is your superpower. So, buckle up; we're diving deep into the realm of verification.

Imagine having a pair of truth goggles that could cut through the noise and reveal the naked truth. Well, get ready to wear those goggles, because we're introducing you to the fascinating world of fact-checking—a skill that will empower you to navigate the sea of information with confidence.

Why Fact-Checking Matters
Before we dive into the how, let's understand the why. In a world where misinformation spreads faster than wildfire, fact-checking is your shield. It's not about being a human lie detector; it's about equipping yourself with

the tools to sift through the chaos and find the golden nuggets of truth.

The Three C's of Fact-Checking

Fact-checking is not reserved for the elite; it's a skill anyone can master. We'll break it down into three easy-to-remember C's:

1. Claim Examination:

Start by scrutinizing the claim at hand. Is it too good to be true? Too outrageous to believe? Break it down into smaller chunks, and let's examine each piece under the microscope of skepticism.

Troubleshooting Tip: Feeling overwhelmed? Take it one step at a time. Address each component of the claim individually for a clearer perspective.

2. Context Analysis:

Context is the unsung hero of fact-checking. Often, misleading information thrives in the absence of context. Explore the who, what, when, where, and why surrounding the claim. The devil's in the details, and context is your angelic ally.

Troubleshooting Tip: Context not adding up? Dig deeper. Seek additional sources or background information to piece together the puzzle.

3. Credibility Check:

Every claim has a backstory, and every source has a history. Evaluate the credibility of the source making the claim. Does it have a track record of honesty, or is it the boy who cried wolf? A credible source adds weight to a claim; an unreliable one sends you back to the drawing board.

Troubleshooting Tip: Doubting the credibility? Cross-reference with trusted sources or fact-checking websites to validate or debunk the claim.

The Fact-Checking Toolkit

Now that you're acquainted with the three C's, let's fill your fact-checking toolkit with a few essentials:

1. Reverse Image Search:

Uncover the origins of an image and verify its authenticity using reverse image search engines.

2. Fact-Checking Websites:

Lean on the expertise of dedicated fact-checking websites. They've got your back when it comes to dissecting claims and separating fact from fiction.

3. Logical Reasoning:

Engage your critical thinking skills. Does the claim align with what you already know? Does it defy the laws of logic? Trust your instincts.

Key Takeaways:

1. Fact-checking is your superpower against misinformation.
2. The Three C's: Claim Examination, Context Analysis, and Credibility Check.
3. Your fact-checking toolkit includes reverse image search, fact-checking websites, and logical reasoning.

Next Steps:

Practice fact-checking on a few claims or articles. Soon, you'll wield the truth goggles with the finesse of a seasoned detective. Get ready to be your own fact-checking hero!

Using Fact-Checking Websites and Tools

Welcome back, truth crusaders! In this segment, we're delving into two vital components of your truth arsenal: "Using Fact-Checking Websites and Tools" and "Developing Critical Thinking Skills." Get ready to supercharge your fact-checking prowess and elevate your critical thinking to new heights.

Using Fact-Checking Websites and Tools

Imagine having a sidekick that scours the vast internet landscape for truths and untruths. Well, fact-checking websites are just that, your digital allies in the war against misinformation. Here's your guide on how to make the most of these superhero tools:

1. Choose Reputable Fact-Checking Websites:

Just like choosing a trustworthy sidekick, opt for fact-checking websites with a solid reputation. Websites like Snopes, FactCheck.org, and PolitiFact have earned their stripes in the battle against falsehoods.

Troubleshooting Tip: Unsure about a fact-checking website? Check its own track record and reviews from reliable sources.

2. Cross-Reference with Multiple Sources:

Fact-checking websites are your initial line of defense, but it's always wise to cross-reference. Multiple sources singing the same tune? You're on solid ground. Divergent opinions? Time to investigate further.

Troubleshooting Tip: Conflicting information? Dive deeper into the nuances. Sometimes, the truth lies in the details.

3. Utilize Fact-Checking Tools:

Embrace the tools designed to make fact-checking a breeze. Browser extensions, plugins, and online tools can quickly flag potential misinformation, saving you time and sparing you from the headache of deciphering every claim manually.

Troubleshooting Tip: Tools not providing clear results? Understand their limitations and always double-check critical claims.

4. Fact-Check in Real Time:

The internet moves at warp speed, and misinformation spreads like wildfire. Use fact-checking websites and tools in real-time to nip falsehoods in the bud. Be the first line of defense against the viral spread of untruths.

Developing Critical Thinking Skills

Now, let's talk about your ultimate superpower, critical thinking. It's not just about fact-checking; it's about equipping yourself with the mental armor to discern truth from fiction in every aspect of life.

1. Question Everything:

Channel your inner curiosity. Don't accept information at face value. Question the motives behind the message, the potential biases, and the credibility of the source.

Troubleshooting Tip: Feeling overwhelmed? Start by questioning one piece of information each day. It's like flexing your critical thinking muscles.

2. Consider Multiple Perspectives:

Critical thinking is a panoramic view, not a narrow snapshot. Embrace diverse perspectives to enrich your understanding. It's not about agreeing with everyone; it's about understanding the full spectrum of opinions.

Troubleshooting Tip: Struggling with diverse perspectives? Engage in respectful conversations with people holding different views to broaden your understanding.

3. Fact vs. Opinion Analysis:

Learn to distinguish between facts and opinions. Facts are concrete, while opinions are subjective. Practice sorting through information by categorizing it into these two buckets.

Troubleshooting Tip: Confused by a statement? Break it down into factual claims and subjective opinions to analyze them separately.

4. Be Aware of Cognitive Biases:

We all have biases, it's part of being human. Acknowledge your biases and be aware of how they might influence your perception. It's the first step towards mitigating their impact.

Troubleshooting Tip: Caught in a bias trap? Pause, reflect, and consciously consider alternative viewpoints.

Congratulations, truth champions! Armed with fact-checking websites, tools, and honed critical thinking skills, you're ready to face the information battlefield with unwavering confidence.

Key Takeaways:
1. Choose reputable fact-checking websites and tools.
2. Cross-reference information from multiple sources.
3. Leverage fact-checking tools for efficiency.

4. Develop critical thinking skills for a holistic approach to truth-seeking.

Next Steps:
Explore fact-checking websites and tools in action. Challenge yourself to critically analyze one piece of information every day. Your journey to becoming a master truth-seeker is gaining momentum!

Chapter 4
Navigating Social Media

Social Media and the Spread of Misinformation

Hello, digital explorers! Welcome to the heart of our quest, Chapter 4, where we set sail into the dynamic realm of social media. In this chapter, we'll unravel the intricacies of "Social Media and the Spread of Misinformation." Ready to surf the waves of information without getting caught in the undertow of falsehoods? Let's dive in!

Social Media and the Spread of Misinformation
Social media, our modern town square, where information flows like a river. But beware, for in these virtual streets, misinformation can spread like wildfire. Let's equip ourselves with the tools and insights to navigate this bustling marketplace of ideas.

Step 1: The Fast and the Furious Flow of Information
Social media moves at the speed of light. Information can go viral before you finish your morning coffee. It's thrilling, but it also means misinformation can spread

like wildfire. So, buckle up and get ready for a bumpy ride.

Troubleshooting Tip: Feeling overwhelmed by the speed? Take a breath. Pause before sharing and verify information before joining the race.

Step 2: The Echo Chamber Effect

Social media often creates echo chambers, spaces where our beliefs are echoed back to us. It feels cozy but can lead to the reinforcement of misinformation. Be wary of becoming a parrot; challenge your own beliefs.

Troubleshooting Tip: Stuck in an echo chamber? Diversify your social media diet. Follow accounts with diverse perspectives to break the echo.

Step 3: The Virality Conundrum

Just because something's popular doesn't mean it's true. Virality is not synonymous with accuracy. Misinformation often rides the wave of popularity. Before you hop on the bandwagon, ensure it's not headed for the cliff.

Troubleshooting Tip: Tempted to share? Verify first. Check the facts before contributing to the viral whirlwind.

Step 4: The Source Scrutiny Dance

On social media, everyone's a publisher. Be discerning about the sources you trust. A catchy profile name and a slick avatar don't guarantee credibility. Investigate the source before considering the information as gospel.

Troubleshooting Tip: Unsure about a source? Fact-check it, and check if others you trust share similar information.

Step 5: The Misleading Visuals Spectacle

A picture may be worth a thousand words, but it can also tell a thousand lies. Misleading visuals are a common tactic on social media. Don't let your eyes be deceived; scrutinize images and videos with a detective's eye.

Troubleshooting Tip: Skeptical about an image? Reverse image search it or consult fact-checking websites for verification.

Step 6: The Comment Section Pitfall

The comment section is a double-edged sword. It's a treasure trove of diverse opinions, but it can also be a breeding ground for misinformation. Engage with caution, fact-check claims, and don't be swayed by the loudest voice in the room.

Troubleshooting Tip: Feeling overwhelmed in the comments? Filter through the noise. Focus on constructive discussions and fact-based arguments.

Navigating social media is like exploring a bustling marketplace, exciting yet potentially treacherous. Armed with these insights, you're ready to navigate the labyrinth of information, avoiding the pitfalls of misinformation along the way.

Key Takeaways:
1. Social media is a fast-paced information highway.
2. Beware of echo chambers and seek diverse perspectives.
3. Virality doesn't guarantee accuracy, verify before sharing.
4. Scrutinize the source's credibility on social media.
5. Be cautious of misleading visuals and fact-check them.
6. Approach the comment section with a critical eye.

Next Steps:
Apply these steps during your next social media scroll. Share reliable information, fact-check claims, and contribute to a healthier online ecosystem. Your journey as a savvy digital navigator is well underway!

Tips for Evaluating Information on Social Platforms

Welcome, fellow truth-seekers, to the battlefield of social media where facts and fictions engage in an epic showdown. In this section, we'll equip you with the armor and weapons you need for the fight, here are "Tips for Evaluating Information on Social Platforms."

Tip 1: The Source Scrutiny Ritual

Before you take that information at face value, perform the Source Scrutiny Ritual. Investigate the author or the account sharing the content. Is it a credible source, or just a digital pied piper leading you astray? Look for verifiable credentials and a history of trustworthy contributions.

Troubleshooting Tip: Source raising eyebrows? Cross-reference with reliable outlets or fact-checking websites to validate.

Tip 2: The Cross-Verification Tango

Never put all your trust eggs in one social media basket. Cross-verify information by consulting multiple sources. If the same story is making rounds across diverse platforms, you're likely onto something real. Consistency is the key; let it open the door to truth.

Troubleshooting Tip: Divergent information? Delve deeper into the nuances. Sometimes, the truth lies in the details.

Tip 3: The Fact-Check Samba

Before hitting the "share" button, make fact-checking your dance partner. Fact-checking websites are your trusty companions in this quest. They'll separate the wheat from the chaff, the facts from the fiction, ensuring your social media dance floor is truth-filled.

Troubleshooting Tip: Doubting the fact-check? Verify the fact-checker. Reliable fact-checkers have transparent methodologies and cite their sources.

Tip 4: The Visual Verification Ballet

Misleading visuals love to pirouette on social media. Don't let them fool you. Engage in the Visual Verification Ballet. Scrutinize images and videos like a discerning judge at a talent show. Look for inconsistencies, check for context, and don't let illusions sway your judgment.

Troubleshooting Tip: Suspicious visuals? Use reverse image search tools to unveil their true identity.[1]

Combating Echo Chambers and Confirmation Bias

Now, let's tackle the formidable foes, Echo Chambers and Confirmation Bias. These stealthy adversaries thrive on social media, shaping our perceptions and narrowing our worldview. But fear not; we have the antidote.

Antidote 1: The Diverse Feed Diet

Break free from the echo chamber's clutches by curating a diverse feed diet. Follow accounts and platforms that offer a range of perspectives. Diversity is your secret weapon against the monotonous hum of a singular narrative.

Troubleshooting Tip: Stuck in an echo chamber? Hit the "unfollow" button on accounts that echo your existing beliefs. Embrace diversity.

Antidote 2: The Contrarian Challenge

Challenge yourself with the Contrarian Challenge. Seek out opinions that run counter to your own. Engage in respectful discussions with individuals who hold different views. It's not about changing your mind; it's about enriching your perspective.

Troubleshooting Tip: Struggling with opposing views? Approach discussions with empathy and a genuine desire to understand.

Antidote 3: The Pause and Reflect Pause

Combat confirmation bias with the Pause and Reflect Pause. When you encounter information that aligns with your existing beliefs, take a moment to pause and reflect. Challenge yourself to question the validity of the information objectively.

Troubleshooting Tip: Falling into the confirmation bias trap? Actively seek out opposing viewpoints to balance your perspective.

Armed with these tips and antidotes, you're now a formidable force in the world of social media. Navigate the information landscape with wisdom, and let the truth prevail in the digital wilderness.

Key Takeaways:

1. Scrutinize the credibility of the source sharing information.

2. Cross-verify information by consulting multiple sources.

3. Embrace fact-checking as your social media dance partner.

4. Engage in the Visual Verification Ballet for images and videos.

5. Combat echo chambers by diversifying your social media feed.

6. Challenge confirmation bias through diverse perspectives and self-reflection.

Next Steps:
Apply these tips to your social media interactions. Share reliable information, engage in diverse discussions, and be the beacon of truth in your digital community. Your journey as a social media truth-seeker is well underway!

Chapter 5

Verifying Online Information

Cross-Referencing Sources

Greetings, vigilant truth-seekers! In Chapter 5, we embark on a journey deep into the heart of online information verification. Here, we unveil the art of "Cross-Referencing Sources," a technique that will empower you to navigate the vast digital ocean with confidence.

Verifying Online Information

In the digital age, information is abundant, but truth can be elusive. It's time to don your detective hat and unveil the secrets of verifying online information. Buckle up; it's about to get exciting!

1. The Multisource Approach:

Just as a mosaic is created by assembling various pieces, the truth often emerges by piecing together information from multiple sources. Cross-referencing involves consulting various outlets to build a comprehensive picture of the story. One source might offer a piece of the puzzle, but the complete picture emerges when you gather insights from different perspectives.

Troubleshooting Tip: Conflicting information? Look for common ground and scrutinize the details where opinions diverge.

2. Diverse Media Outlets:

Diversify your news intake. Cross-reference information across a spectrum of media outlets with different biases and perspectives. Mainstream, alternative, local, and international sources can contribute valuable nuances to the narrative. A diverse media diet ensures you're not confined to a single echo chamber.

Troubleshooting Tip: Feeling overwhelmed? Create a list of trusted outlets representing various viewpoints to streamline your cross-referencing process.

3. Timeline Alignment:

Time is the unsung hero of information verification. Cross-referencing timelines helps establish the chronology of events. Ensure that the information aligns with the temporal sequence of the story. Misinformation often thrives by distorting the sequence of events.

Troubleshooting Tip: Timeline discrepancies? Investigate the sequence of events by consulting reliable historical records or eyewitness accounts.

4. Expert Consensus:

Seek the consensus of experts. Cross-referencing with experts in the field can provide a crucial layer of validation. Experts bring a depth of knowledge and experience that can substantiate or debunk information. Peer-reviewed journals, interviews, and recognized authorities can serve as beacons of credibility.

Troubleshooting Tip: Disputes among experts? Delve into the credentials, methodologies, and motivations of the conflicting parties to discern the more credible stance.

5. Fact-Checking Organizations:

Fact-checking organizations are your allies in the truth-seeking quest. Cross-referencing with their findings adds an extra layer of verification. These organizations employ rigorous methodologies to scrutinize claims and unearth the factual foundation beneath the surface.

Troubleshooting Tip: Fact-checking controversies? Investigate the fact-checking organization's reputation, transparency, and adherence to ethical standards.

Key Takeaways:
1. Cross-referencing involves consulting multiple sources to build a comprehensive understanding.
2. Diversify your media intake, incorporating outlets with different biases and perspectives.
3. Align timelines to establish the chronology of events.
4. Seek the consensus of experts to validate or debunk information.
5. Fact-checking organizations serve as reliable allies in the verification process.

Next Steps:
Practice cross-referencing on a variety of news stories or claims. As you assemble the pieces of the truth mosaic, you'll become adept at navigating the intricate landscape of online information verification. Get ready to be a master of discernment in the digital age!

Utilizing Reverse Image Searches

Greetings, digital detectives! In Chapter 6, we're delving into the fascinating world of "Utilizing Reverse Image Searches." This technique is your secret weapon for uncovering the truth behind images and visuals circulating in the vast online landscape.

1. The Image Verification Ballet:

Just as a dancer scrutinizes every move, you'll perform the Image Verification Ballet. Reverse image searches allow you to track down the origins of an image by submitting it to search engines. Google Images, TinEye, and other tools become your dance floor, revealing the true identity of visuals.

Troubleshooting Tip: Ambiguous results? Experiment with different search engines and refine your query to enhance accuracy.

2. Detecting Manipulation and Plagiarism:

Reverse image searches unveil the smoke and mirrors of visual deception. Are you suspicious of Photoshop wizardry or concerned about potential plagiarism? By cross-referencing visuals, you expose manipulated images and discover if someone else is claiming ownership of the same visual masterpiece.

Troubleshooting Tip: Unsettled by conflicting information? Dig deeper into the sources and consult experts to verify the authenticity of the visuals.

3. Tracking Down Original Sources:

Images often embark on a digital journey, appearing on various websites and platforms. Reverse image searches are your compass, guiding you back to the original source. Whether it's a viral meme or a gripping photograph, tracing its footsteps allows you to confirm its authenticity and context.

Troubleshooting Tip: Hitting dead ends? Explore alternative search terms or consider refining your search based on additional contextual information.

4. Spotting Deepfakes and Altered Visuals:

In the era of deepfakes and digital manipulations, visual authenticity is crucial. Reverse image searches assist you in unmasking altered visuals, ensuring that what you see is what actually occurred. By comparing the image with verified sources, you become a vigilant guardian against visual deception.

Troubleshooting Tip: Skeptical of a flawless image? Consult deepfake detection tools or seek expert opinions for confirmation.

Confirming Information Reliability

Now that we've mastered the art of reverse image searches, let's tackle the broader landscape of "Confirming Information Reliability." This chapter equips you with the tools and mindset needed to ensure the accuracy and trustworthiness of the information you encounter.

1. The Credibility Check:

Begin your reliability quest with a Credibility Check. Evaluate the source providing the information. Is it a reputable news outlet, an expert in the field, or a reliable organization? The credibility of the source serves as a solid foundation for confirming the reliability of the information.

Troubleshooting Tip: Doubting the credibility? Explore the source's track record, affiliations, and motivations.

2. Cross-Verification Symphony:

Just as an orchestra harmonizes different instruments, you'll perform the Cross-Verification Symphony. Validate information by consulting multiple reliable sources. Consistency among trustworthy outlets solidifies the reliability of the information, transforming it from a single note into a symphony of truth.

Troubleshooting Tip: Divergent information? Seek common ground among reliable sources and investigate the nuances where they differ.

3. The Expert Opinion Ensemble:

For complex topics, enlist the Expert Opinion Ensemble. Seek the insights of professionals, specialists, or recognized authorities in the relevant field. Their expertise adds a layer of validation, confirming the accuracy of information through the lens of subject matter experts.

Troubleshooting Tip: Conflicting expert opinions? Investigate the methodologies, biases, and motivations of the experts to discern the more credible stance.

4. Fact-Checking Choreography:

Dance with the Fact-Checking Choreography to confirm information reliability. Fact-checking organizations are your dance partners in this endeavor. Their meticulous fact-checking methodologies and transparent processes help separate fact from fiction, ensuring the accuracy of the information you encounter.

Troubleshooting Tip: Fact-checking controversies? Scrutinize the fact-checking organization's reputation, methodologies, and adherence to ethical standards.

Chapter 6

Understanding Media Literacy

Media Literacy and its Role in Information Evaluation

Greetings, information navigators! In Chapter 6, we embark on an enlightening exploration into the realm of "Understanding Media Literacy." This chapter is your compass, guiding you through the seas of information, helping you decipher, decode, and discern the nuances of media messages.

1. Decoding the Language of Media:

Media speaks a language of its own, filled with symbols, images, and narratives. Understanding Media Literacy is akin to learning a new language. It involves deciphering the nuances of visual and written communication, identifying biases, and unraveling the hidden messages within media content.

Navigational Tip: Start by breaking down visuals and headlines. Question the choices made in framing stories and portraying images.

2. Navigating Media Bias:

Media outlets, like individuals, have their own perspectives and biases. Media Literacy acts as your compass, helping you navigate through the biases inherent in news reporting and storytelling. By recognizing these biases, you can approach information with a discerning eye, distinguishing between fact and opinion.

Navigational Tip: Consume news from a variety of sources to gain a more comprehensive understanding of different perspectives.

3. Critical Consumption Practices:

Media Literacy empowers you with critical consumption practices. It's not just about what media presents; it's about how you consume it. By actively engaging with media content, asking questions, and fact-checking claims, you become an active participant rather than a passive recipient of information.

Navigational Tip: Develop a habit of questioning information. Ask yourself who benefits from a particular narrative and what might be omitted.

4. Analyzing Media Techniques:
Media utilizes a variety of techniques to convey messages effectively. Media Literacy equips you with the tools to analyze these techniques, whether it's the use of persuasive language, visual elements, or framing. By understanding these strategies, you can decipher the intention behind the messaging.

Navigational Tip: Deconstruct advertisements, news articles, and social media posts to identify the techniques employed in shaping public opinion.

Media Literacy and its Role in Information Evaluation

1. Empowering Critical Thinkers:
At its core, Media Literacy empowers individuals to become critical thinkers. It encourages you to question, analyze, and evaluate the information presented by media outlets. This critical thinking stance enables you to filter through the noise, separating reliable information from misinformation.

Evaluation Insight: Embrace skepticism as a tool for inquiry. Don't accept information at face value; challenge it.

2. Guarding Against Manipulation:
Media Literacy serves as a shield against manipulation. By understanding how media messages are crafted and the potential for manipulation, you become less susceptible to being swayed by misleading narratives. It's your defense mechanism against the subtle art of persuasion.

Evaluation Insight: Be aware of emotional triggers in media content. Question narratives that evoke strong emotions without providing factual evidence.

3. Promoting Informed Citizenship:
Media Literacy is a cornerstone of informed citizenship. In a democratic society, an informed citizenry is essential. Media Literacy fosters a community of individuals who not only consume information responsibly but also actively contribute to a well-informed public discourse.

Evaluation Insight: Engage in constructive conversations based on well-researched information. Share reliable sources and encourage media literacy in your community.

4. Building Resilience Against Misinformation:

In the era of misinformation, Media Literacy is your armor. It builds resilience by arming you with the skills to identify, question, and reject false information. By cultivating a media-literate mindset, you become a savvy navigator, adept at steering through the misinformation storms that may arise in the digital landscape.

Evaluation Insight: Develop a habit of cross-referencing information, fact-checking claims, and consulting diverse sources to build a robust defense against misinformation.

As we delve into the heart of Media Literacy, remember that it's not just about consuming media, it's about understanding the language it speaks, recognizing its biases, and actively participating in the discourse it shapes. With Media Literacy as your guiding star, you're well-equipped to sail through the information seas, discerning truth from the vast ocean of messages that surround us. Happy navigating!

Analyzing News and Media Outlets

Hello, discerning readers! Here, we embark on a journey of insight, focusing on "Analyzing News and Media Outlets." This chapter is your guide to becoming a critical consumer of information, understanding the nuances of news sources, and navigating the diverse landscape of media outlets.

1. Understanding Editorial Standards:

Every news outlet has its own editorial standards that shape the content it produces. These standards influence the choice of stories, language used, and the overall tone. By understanding a media outlet's editorial stance, you gain insight into its perspective and potential biases.

Insightful Tip: Explore a media outlet's mission statement, editorial guidelines, and policies to understand its journalistic values.

2. Examining Ownership and Funding:

Media outlets are not immune to external influences, and examining ownership and funding sources can reveal potential conflicts of interest. Knowing who owns and funds a news organization provides context to its coverage and helps you assess its independence.

Insightful Tip: Investigate the ownership structure and financial backers of a media outlet to uncover potential biases.

3. Assessing Journalistic Integrity:

Journalistic integrity is the backbone of reliable news reporting. Analyze how well a media outlet adheres to ethical journalism practices, including fact-checking, unbiased reporting, and transparency. Outlets with a commitment to journalistic integrity are more likely to provide accurate information.

Insightful Tip: Look for media outlets that are members of professional journalism organizations and adhere to established ethical guidelines.

4. Diversity of Voices and Perspectives:

A robust news outlet offers a diversity of voices and perspectives. Analyze the range of contributors, journalists, and experts featured in a media outlet's content. A variety of perspectives enhances the depth and credibility of news coverage.

Insightful Tip: Explore the backgrounds and expertise of journalists to ensure a diverse range of voices in the reporting.

Promoting Responsible Media Consumption

1. Curate Your Information Diet:

Just as you curate your meals for a balanced diet, curate your information intake. Consume news from a variety of sources with different perspectives. A diverse information diet helps you develop a well-rounded understanding of events and issues.

Responsible Practice: Regularly assess your news sources and actively seek out new perspectives to avoid information echo chambers.

2. Verify Before Sharing:

The responsibility of a media consumer extends to sharing information. Before hitting the share button, verify the accuracy of the information. Misinformation can spread rapidly, and by ensuring your contributions are factual, you become a responsible participant in the information ecosystem.

Responsible Practice: Use fact-checking tools and consult reliable sources before sharing news or information on social media.

3. Engage in Constructive Discourse:

Responsible media consumption involves engaging in constructive discourse. Encourage open conversations, share diverse perspectives, and contribute to a healthy exchange of ideas. By fostering respectful discussions, you contribute to a more informed and engaged society.

Responsible Practice: Approach discussions with empathy, actively listen to different viewpoints, and contribute thoughtfully to public discourse.

4. Support Independent Journalism:

Independent journalism is a cornerstone of a vibrant democracy. Support media outlets that prioritize journalistic integrity, independence, and a commitment to truth. By subscribing to or financially supporting reputable news sources, you contribute to the sustainability of quality journalism.

Responsible Practice: Consider subscribing to news outlets, contributing to crowdfunding campaigns, or supporting nonprofit journalism organizations.

In our quest for information, let's not only be consumers but responsible stewards of the media landscape. By analyzing news outlets and promoting responsible media consumption, we contribute to a more informed, diverse, and resilient society. Happy reading!

Chapter 7

Critical Thinking in the Era of Misinformation

Strengthening Analytical Skills

Greetings, fellow truth-seekers! In Chapter 7, we dive deep into the vital skill of "Critical Thinking in the Era of Misinformation." This chapter is your compass through the information wilderness, equipping you with the cognitive tools to navigate the complexities of our digital age.

1. The Power of Questioning:

Critical thinking begins with the power of questioning. In the era of misinformation, cultivate a habit of asking probing questions about the information you encounter. Who is the source? What is their agenda? Why is this information presented in a particular way? By questioning, you peel back the layers of deception.

Analytical Tip: Challenge assumptions, scrutinize motives, and question the narrative behind the information.

2. Navigating Cognitive Biases:

Our minds are susceptible to cognitive biases that can lead us astray. Critical thinking involves recognizing and navigating these biases. Whether it's confirmation bias, where we favor information that confirms our preexisting beliefs, or availability bias, where we rely on readily available information, understanding these biases is crucial.

Analytical Tip: Actively seek out information that challenges your existing beliefs, and be aware of the limitations of personal experiences in forming opinions.

3. Analyzing Source Credibility:

Strengthen your analytical skills by honing in on source credibility. Evaluate the reliability of the sources providing information. Is it a reputable news outlet, an expert in the field, or an anonymous online entity? Critical thinking demands a careful examination of the source's track record, expertise, and potential biases.

Analytical Tip: Verify the credentials, check for potential conflicts of interest, and cross-reference information from multiple reliable sources.

4. Connecting the Dots:

Critical thinking involves connecting the dots between pieces of information. Misinformation often thrives in isolated fragments. By piecing together a comprehensive narrative, you unveil the broader context and identify inconsistencies that may indicate misinformation.

Analytical Tip: Create mental or written maps to connect related information, helping you see the bigger picture and identify gaps or contradictions.

Strengthening Analytical Skills

1. Diversify Your Information Diet:
Strengthening analytical skills involves exposing yourself to diverse perspectives. Diversify your information diet by consuming content from various sources, representing different viewpoints. This not only broadens your understanding but also enhances your ability to critically analyze contrasting narratives.

Strengthening Practice: Regularly explore news outlets, podcasts, and online platforms that offer diverse perspectives on current events.

2. Practice Active Listening:
Critical thinking extends to active listening, engaging with information in a thoughtful, receptive manner. Whether in conversations, presentations, or media consumption, actively listen to different viewpoints. This

practice enhances your ability to discern nuances and evaluate information with a discerning ear.

Strengthening Practice: Engage in discussions with individuals holding diverse opinions, and practice summarizing their perspectives to ensure understanding.

3. Evaluate Arguments Systematically:

Analytical skills are honed by systematically evaluating arguments. Break down complex information into manageable parts, assess the validity of claims, and identify the evidence supporting or refuting those claims. This systematic approach strengthens your ability to separate logic from fallacy.

Strengthening Practice: When faced with a persuasive argument, deconstruct it into premises and conclusions, and evaluate each component independently.

4. Continuous Learning and Adaptation:

The information landscape is ever-evolving, requiring continuous learning and adaptation. Strengthen your analytical skills by staying informed about new developments, emerging technologies, and evolving narratives. A nimble and adaptive mind is a powerful tool against misinformation.

Strengthening Practice: Set aside time for regular learning, explore new subjects, and stay informed about advancements in media and technology.

In the era of misinformation, critical thinking is your shield against deception. By questioning, analyzing, and strengthening your analytical skills, you become a vigilant guardian of truth. As you embark on this journey of critical thinking, remember that the pursuit of knowledge is a continuous process, one that empowers you to navigate the complex landscape of information with confidence and clarity. Happy critical thinking!

Questioning Assumptions and Biases

Greetings, inquisitive minds! In Chapter 8, we delve into the art of "Questioning Assumptions and Biases." This chapter is your guide to wielding the tools of critical thinking with precision, unraveling hidden assumptions, and navigating the intricate terrain of biases that shape our perceptions.

1. *Unraveling Assumptions:*

Our minds often operate on autopilot, driven by unspoken assumptions. Critical thinking demands that we bring these assumptions into the light. What beliefs do we take for granted? Are there hidden premises guiding our thoughts? By unraveling assumptions, we create space for conscious, deliberate thinking.

Inquiry Insight: Actively question the foundations of your beliefs. Ask yourself why you hold certain assumptions and consider alternative perspectives.

2. *Interrogating Implicit Biases:*

Biases, often lurking beneath the surface, shape our judgments without our conscious awareness. Critical thinking involves interrogating these implicit biases. Examine your predispositions and prejudices, recognizing how they influence your perceptions.

Unmasking these biases is the first step toward unbiased thinking.

Inquiry Insight: Reflect on your reactions and judgments. Are they influenced by preconceived notions or stereotypes? Challenge these biases.

3. Challenging Status Quo Beliefs:

Critical thinking is a rebel against the status quo. It encourages us to challenge long-held beliefs and question the legitimacy of established norms. What may seem unquestionable might hold hidden assumptions. By challenging status quo beliefs, we foster intellectual independence and a deeper understanding of the world.

Inquiry Insight: Identify beliefs you've never questioned. Ask yourself why you hold them and consider alternative perspectives that may challenge the status quo.

4. Examining Cultural and Contextual Influences:

Our cultural and contextual surroundings shape our assumptions and biases. Critical thinking requires an examination of these influences. How has culture molded our beliefs? What contextual factors contribute to our biases? By understanding these influences, we gain insight into the multifaceted nature of our thought processes.

Inquiry Insight: Explore how your cultural background and context contribute to your assumptions and biases. Consider how others from different backgrounds might perceive the same information.

Applying Critical Thinking to Everyday Information

1. Media Consumption with a Critical Lens:
In the age of information overload, applying critical thinking to media consumption is paramount. Scrutinize news articles, social media posts, and advertisements. Question the motives behind information dissemination, assess the credibility of sources, and be vigilant against the influence of biases.

Application Tip: Before accepting information, analyze the source, cross-reference facts, and consider potential biases that may shape the narrative.

2. Evaluating Personal Decision-Making:
Critical thinking extends to personal decision-making. Evaluate the assumptions guiding your decisions. Are they based on evidence, or do they rely on untested beliefs? By subjecting your decision-making process to critical scrutiny, you enhance the quality of choices and minimize the impact of unconscious biases.

Application Tip: Before making decisions, articulate the assumptions behind each option, assess their validity, and consider alternative perspectives.

3. Constructive Dialogue and Empathy:

Engaging in constructive dialogue demands a foundation of critical thinking. Listen actively, challenge assumptions diplomatically, and approach conversations with empathy. By applying critical thinking in dialogue, you foster an environment where diverse perspectives are considered, and assumptions are openly questioned.

Application Tip: Practice active listening, ask clarifying questions, and be open to revising your views based on new information.

4. Problem-Solving with Analytical Rigor:

In everyday problem-solving, apply critical thinking with analytical rigor. Break down complex issues into manageable components, question underlying assumptions, and consider alternative solutions. By approaching problems with a critical lens, you enhance your ability to navigate challenges effectively.

Application Tip: Systematically analyze problems, question assumptions influencing potential solutions, and explore a range of approaches before settling on a decision.

Chapter 8

Combating Disinformation Campaigns

Recognizing the Tactics of Disinformation

Greetings, truth defenders! In Chapter 8, we embark on a mission to tackle the ever-present challenge of "Combating Disinformation Campaigns." This chapter equips you with the tools to discern truth from fiction, navigate the murky waters of disinformation, and become a vigilant guardian against manipulative campaigns.

1. Understanding Disinformation:

Disinformation, the deliberate spread of false or misleading information, is a persistent threat in our interconnected world. Understanding the anatomy of disinformation is the first step in combating it. Disinformation often serves hidden agendas, aiming to manipulate public opinion, sow discord, or achieve political objectives.

Vigilance Tip: Stay informed about ongoing disinformation campaigns and be aware of the potential motives behind them.

2. The Role of Social Media:

Social media platforms have become battlegrounds for disinformation campaigns. Manipulative actors exploit the rapid dissemination of information on these platforms to amplify falsehoods. Recognizing the role of social media in disinformation allows you to approach information with a discerning eye.

Vigilance Tip: Be cautious of information shared on social media platforms and verify claims before sharing or believing them.

3. Targeting Vulnerabilities:

Disinformation campaigns often target specific vulnerabilities within societies. Whether exploiting pre-existing biases, capitalizing on social divides, or tapping into emotional triggers, recognizing these vulnerabilities is crucial. By understanding how disinformation exploits weaknesses, you become better equipped to resist its influence.

Vigilance Tip: Reflect on your own biases and emotional responses to information. Disrupt the cycle by actively seeking diverse perspectives.

Recognizing the Tactics of Disinformation

1. False Narratives and Manipulated Facts:
Disinformation thrives on false narratives and manipulated facts. Be vigilant against sensational stories that lack credible sources or present information out of context. Recognizing these tactics involves scrutinizing the narrative's consistency and verifying the accuracy of presented facts.

Recognition Insight: Question narratives that evoke strong emotions and fact-check information from multiple reliable sources.

2. Deepfakes and Altered Media:
The rise of deepfakes and manipulated media presents a new frontier in disinformation. Recognizing altered visuals or fabricated audio is essential. Disinformation campaigns may use these techniques to deceive and mislead, so developing skills to identify manipulated media is paramount.

Recognition Insight: Utilize reverse image searches and fact-checking tools to verify the authenticity of media content.

3. Impersonation and Fake Accounts:

Disinformation often involves the creation of fake personas or accounts to spread misleading content. Recognizing impersonation tactics involves scrutinizing account details, evaluating posting patterns, and verifying the authenticity of online entities.

Recognition Insight: Be cautious of unsolicited friend requests, followers, or messages. Verify the legitimacy of online accounts before engaging with them.

4. Cherry-Picking and Selective Quoting:

Disinformation campaigns excel at cherry-picking information to suit their narratives. Recognize selective quoting and manipulation of context by seeking out the complete picture. Be wary of quotes taken out of context or information presented in isolation.

Recognition Insight: Investigate the source of quotes, review the broader context, and question the intent behind selectively presented information.

In the battle against disinformation, your vigilance is the key to victory. By understanding the tactics of disinformation campaigns and honing your skills in recognizing manipulation, you become a formidable force against falsehoods. Stay alert, question narratives, and together, let's combat the spread of disinformation in our information landscape. Happy truth-seeking!

Strategies for Resisting Manipulation

Greetings, guardians of truth! In Chapter 9, we embark on a journey to fortify our defenses against manipulation and uphold the banner of "Strategies for Resisting Manipulation." This chapter empowers you with practical tools to navigate the treacherous waters of misinformation, fostering resilience and promoting information integrity.

1. Cultivating Digital Literacy:

Digital literacy is your armor in the battle against manipulation. Cultivate a deep understanding of how digital platforms operate, from algorithms to data privacy. Being digitally literate enables you to navigate online spaces with confidence, discerning between genuine content and manipulative tactics.

Defense Strategy: Stay informed about the evolving digital landscape, and educate yourself on the inner workings of social media platforms and online ecosystems.

2. Questioning Information Sources:

An essential strategy is to question the sources of information. Manipulators often rely on unverified or biased sources. By habitually questioning the reliability and credibility of information sources, you create a robust defense against manipulation.

Defense Strategy: Scrutinize the background, motives, and reputation of information sources. Be wary of anonymous or suspicious sources.

3. Developing Fact-Checking Habits

Fact-checking is a powerful weapon against manipulation. Cultivate the habit of verifying information before accepting or sharing it. Fact-checking websites and tools are valuable allies in the quest for truth, allowing you to confirm the accuracy of claims.

Defense Strategy: Prioritize fact-checking as part of your information consumption routine. Cross-reference information from multiple reputable fact-checking sources.

4. Building Critical Thinking Skills:

Strengthen your critical thinking muscles to resist manipulation. Analyze information with a discerning eye, question assumptions, and consider alternative perspectives. Critical thinking transforms you into an active, independent thinker, less susceptible to the influence of manipulative tactics.

Defense Strategy: Engage in exercises that challenge your critical thinking skills. Question assumptions, evaluate evidence, and analyze information systematically.

Promoting Information Integrity

1. Encouraging Digital Literacy Education:
Information integrity begins with education. Promote digital literacy education in schools, workplaces, and communities. By empowering individuals with the skills to navigate the digital landscape, we collectively contribute to a society less susceptible to manipulation.

Promotion Approach: Advocate for the integration of digital literacy programs in educational curricula. Support initiatives that promote digital literacy awareness.

2. Fostering Open Dialogues:
Create spaces for open dialogues where individuals can share their experiences with misinformation and manipulation. Fostering conversations about digital manipulation reduces stigma and encourages a collective effort toward information integrity.

Promotion Approach: Organize community forums, workshops, or online discussions focused on sharing experiences and strategies for resisting manipulation.

3. Supporting Ethical Journalism:
Ethical journalism is a cornerstone of information integrity. Support news outlets that prioritize journalistic

principles, fact-checking, and transparent reporting. By endorsing ethical journalism, you contribute to the creation of an information ecosystem grounded in truth.

Promotion Approach: Subscribe to and share content from reputable news sources. Encourage media literacy programs that promote ethical journalism practices.

4. *Promoting Accountability for Platforms:*

Advocate for accountability among digital platforms. Encourage social media platforms and online spaces to implement measures that combat manipulation, including transparent algorithms, user-friendly reporting systems, and responsible content moderation.

Promotion Approach: Support initiatives and organizations advocating for responsible practices by digital platforms. Engage in discussions about the responsibilities of online platforms in combatting misinformation.

As we navigate the complexities of the information age, let these strategies for resisting manipulation be your guiding stars. By fortifying our defenses, promoting digital literacy, and championing information integrity, we pave the way for a future where truth prevails over manipulation.

Conclusion

As we reach the conclusion of our journey through the pages of "How to Spot Fake News and Verify Information Online: Essential Skills for Evaluating Sources and Detecting Lies in the Era of Misinformation," it's clear that we've embarked on a quest for truth in the vast, sometimes treacherous, landscape of information.

In our exploration, we've donned the armor of critical thinking, wielded the sword of fact-checking, and built the fortress of digital literacy. Together, we've confronted the challenges posed by misinformation, disinformation campaigns, and the subtle art of manipulation. We've delved into the strategies for resisting manipulation and championing information integrity.

This book is not just a guide; it's a call to action. It's an invitation to be vigilant truth defenders, active participants in the ongoing battle against misinformation. As we navigate the information seas, let the skills cultivated within these pages be your compass, guiding you toward the shores of truth.

Remember, the title of this book is not just a set of words, it's a promise. It's a commitment to empowering you with the essential skills needed to discern fact from fiction, to sift through the noise and find the signal of truth. In the era of misinformation, being equipped with these skills is not just an advantage; it's a necessity.

So, let us carry forward the lessons learned, the strategies embraced, and the principles upheld. Let us be ambassadors of truth, spreading the light of knowledge and critical thinking in a world often clouded by misinformation.

As you close this book, envision yourself as a beacon of clarity in the fog of misinformation, a guardian of truth in the storm of disinformation. The skills you've honed here are not just for personal enlightenment; they are tools for societal change.

Thank you for joining this journey, fellow truth-seekers. May your quest for truth continue, and may the principles within these pages guide you in evaluating sources, detecting lies, and navigating the era of misinformation with confidence and clarity. Happy truth-navigating!

information. Picture yourself confidently deciphering truth from fiction, effortlessly dismantling misleading headlines, and navigating the murky waters of social media with the precision of a seasoned detective. Intrigued? You should be!

In this book, we'll be your trusty sidekick, guiding you through the intricacies of information literacy in a way that's both enlightening and downright entertaining. We'll unveil the secrets of identifying red flags, mastering fact-checking techniques, and developing the kind of critical thinking skills that make misinformation quiver in fear.
Buckle up as we explore the wild terrain of social media, equipping you with the tools to sift through the noise and emerge unscathed. Whether you're a social media maven or just getting the hang of hashtags, we promise to make your online journey a breeze.

But hey, it's not just about debunking myths and separating fact from fiction, it's about empowering you. Together, we'll forge a shield of knowledge that renders misinformation powerless in your presence. And let's be honest, who wouldn't want to be the superhero of truth in this information-packed world?

FOLDS TO POCKE PERFECTION

THE POCKET SQUARE GUIDE FOR EVERY MAN

ALEXIS BURKE